having it all

having it all

now the world is your oyster

edited by sean keogh

Published in the United States in 2008
by Tangent Publications
an imprint of
Axis Publishing Limited
8c Accommodation Road
London NW11 8ED
www.axispublishing.co.uk

Creative Director: Siân Keogh
Editorial Director: Anne Yelland
Designer: Sean Keogh, Simon De Lotz
Production Manager: Jo Ryan

The material in this book has been previously published in:
Follow Your Dreams, Never Mind, Reach For The Stars, That's Life.

ISBN 978-1-904707-69-1

9 8 7 6 5 4 3 2 1

Printed and bound in China

about this book

When you're young, free, and single, you really can have it all: and this is the book that will inspire you to do just that. A collection of go-get-it words of wisdom on effort and success, this is the volume that will inspire you to great things…and all from the comfort of your armchair.

Full of words of advice and inspiration, and beautifully complemented by amusing animal photographs, this is the book to promote effort and inspire success.

about the author

Sean Keogh has worked in publishing for several years, on a variety of books

and magazines covering a wide range of subjects. From the many hundreds of

contributions that were sent to him from all over the world he has selected

those that best sum up the meaning of success.

The faster you run,
the luckier you get.

Those who follow
the crowd are
quickly lost in it.

The harder the conflict, the more glorious the triumph.

The right person is the one who seizes the opportunity.

Procrastination is the grave in which opportunities are buried.

The door of opportunity
is wide open…

…if you are
prepared for it.

You won't hear the knock on the door if you're wearing headphones.

You can't plow a field by turning it over in your mind.

Looking on the bright side never causes eyestrain.

Opportunities are
never lost…

…someone else
will take the ones
you miss.

Hope is a waking dream.

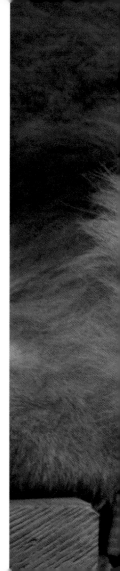

Vision without action
is just a daydream.

The worst thing you
can do is nothing.

The body achieves what
the mind believes.

Seldom does an individual exceed his own expectations.

Have faith in yourself
and your abilities.

Even in the depths of winter, there is an invincible summer.

You can't go back and make
a brand new start, but you
can start over and make
a brand new ending.

Reach up as far as you can and providence will reach down all the way.

It's not what you are that matters, but what you can become.

You don't know how great you can become.

The only victories worth having are those that entailed a hard fight.

A victory without danger is
a triumph without glory.

If you don't climb
the mountain, you
can't view the plain.

Think big. Do good.

Advice is like snow…

…the softer it falls,
the deeper it sinks
into the mind.

Everyone who got where he is has had to begin where he was.

Don't judge each day by the harvest you reap, but by the seeds you sow.

Your altitude is determined by your attitude.

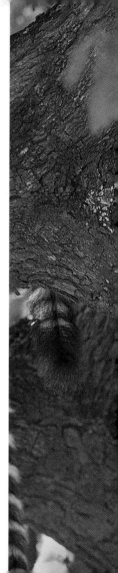

The only limits
to the mind are those
we believe in.

Imagination is the beginning of creation.

There is a time to let things happen, and a time to make things happen.

What you think of yourself
is much more important
than what others think of you.

Do not wait for your
ship to come in…

…swim out to it.

The harder you fall,
the higher you bounce.

You often meet your destiny on the road you've taken to avoid it.

Go out on a limb…

…that's where the fruit is.

Great things are
done by a series
of small things
brought together.

If you're already walking on thin ice, you might as well dance.

No bird soars too high,
if he soars with his
own wings.

A person without a
purpose is like a ship
without a rudder.

Sometimes letting
go is better than
holding on.

Build castles in the air…

…then put foundations under them.

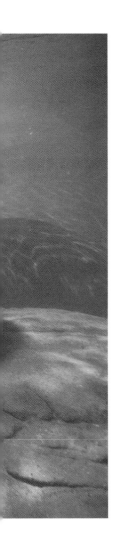

The only way to discover
the limits of the possible
is to go beyond them
into the impossible.

What you become is more important than what you accomplish.

Skillful pilots gain
their reputation from
storms and tempests.

You only hit obstacles when you take your eye off the goal.

You can't win the race
if you don't run.

The best is yet to come.

Good ideas rarely interrupt you.

If there is light
in the soul, there
will be beauty in
the person.

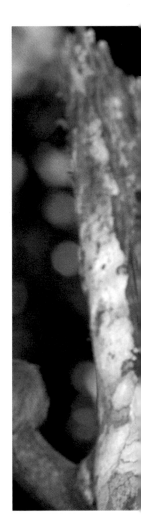

Wisdom is knowing what
path to take next…

…integrity is taking it.

The greater the obstacle,
the more glory in
overcoming it.

Looking at small advantages prevents great affairs from being accomplished.

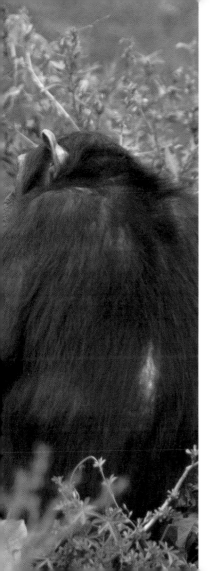

He who asks
is a fool for five
minutes, but he
who does not ask
remains a fool
for life.

This moment is as good as any moment in all eternity.

School's out,
memories past…

…don't ever doubt
our friendship
will last.

The roots of
education are bitter,
but the fruit is sweet.

You can go
in any direction
you choose.

Friendship isn't
a big thing—it's a
million little things.

May your dreams
take you to the corner
of your smiles.

Wherever you go,
go with all your heart.

If you don't have time to do it right, you're going to need time to do it over.

When you feel at your worst is when you get to know yourself best.

Tearing your hair out
only makes you bald.

Dreams are a size too big
so we grow into them.

We must all assume burdens, but we were all born with shoulders.

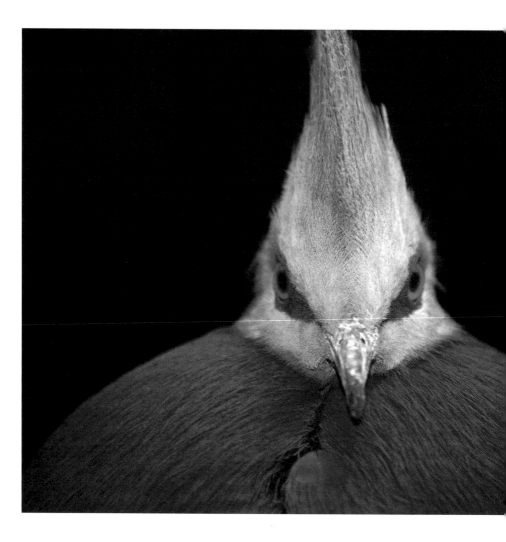

Great ideas need wings and landing gear.

Education is teaching
us how to think,
improving our minds,
so we can think
for ourselves.

Your future's in
good hands…

…your own.

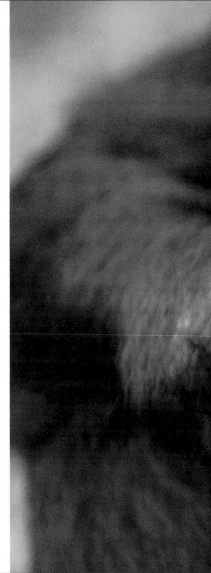

If a place is worth
going to, there are
no shortcuts.

All that stands between
the graduate and the top
of the ladder is the ladder.

Your dream is
your dream: don't let
anybody else steal it.

Dream as if
you'll live forever.

Success is the
ability to
learn, unlearn,
and relearn.

The young graduate
discovers that among the
necessaries of life, the
most important is living.

If you graduated yesterday, and have learned nothing today, you will be uneducated tomorrow.

The school of experience
will repeat a lesson if you
flunk it the first time.

The future lies before you like
a field of driven snow…

…be careful how you tread
it for every step will show.

If at first you
don't succeed,
do it like your
mom told you.

A smart person
knows what to say,
a wise person
knows whether
or not to say it.

Great deeds are usually wrought at great risks.

Education is the
knowledge not of
facts, but of values.

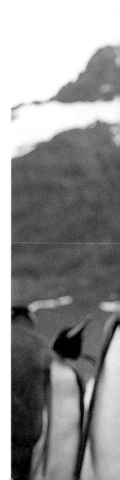

There is just one
life for each of us…

…our own.

Nothing great was
ever accomplished
without passion.

You cannot direct
the wind but you
can adjust the sails.

Do not go where the path may lead; go instead where there is no path and leave a trail.

Everything stems
from a dream.

Meeting again after
moments or lifetimes,
is certain for those
who are friends.

Let your mind be bold.

You can't hold a torch
to light another's path
without brightening
your own.

The ending is
simply a fresh start.

A wise man makes more opportunities than he finds.

There is no need to reach high for the stars…

…they are already within you, just reach deep into yourself.

Behind knowledge
is a seeker.

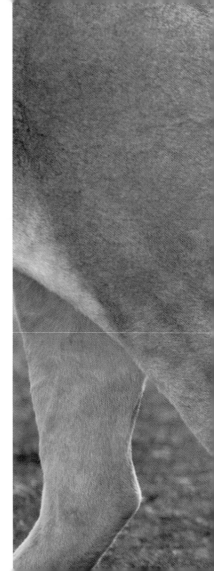

Teachers open the door, but you must enter by yourself.

Goodness does not consist in greatness, but greatness in goodness.

You cannot get to the top
by sitting on your bottom.

The secret of success
is purpose.

Your dreams will
come true if you
have the courage
to follow them.

Education is the
best provision for old age.

Excellence
is an attitude.

May your dreams
take you to the most
special places your
heart has ever known.

Many men can
figure costs,
but few can
measure values.

Do not despise the bottom rungs in the ascent to greatness.

Individuality is
the key to success.

A characteristic of normal children is that they don't act that way very often.

Children seldom misquote you.
In fact, they usually repeat
word for word what you
shouldn't have said.

An optimist makes
opportunities of
his difficulties.

Remain optimistic…

…until they start moving animals in pairs to Cape Canaveral.

No success or failure
is necessarily final.

A dead end street is a place to turn around.

Those parts of the system that you can hit with a hammer are called hardware; the instructions that you can only curse at are called software.

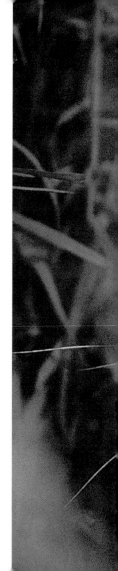

What you don't know takes a lot of explaining to the children.

Back up my hard drive?
How do I put it in reverse?

Experience is what you
get from not having it
when you needed it.

Conscience: Telling your mother what you've done before your brother or sister gets a chance to.

There's nothing wrong with the younger generation that paying taxes won't cure.

There is nothing wrong with today's teenagers that twenty years won't cure.

The average teenager still has all the faults his parents outgrew.

You can tell a child is growing up when he stops asking where he came from and starts refusing to tell where he is going.

You're only young once, but you can stay immature forever.

The purpose of a liberal education is to make you philosophical enough to accept the fact that you will never make much money.

Vacation: A period of travel and relaxation when you take twice the clothes and half the money you need.

There's a very fine line
between fishing and
standing on the shore
like an idiot.

Many people quit looking for work when they find a job.

The brain starts working the moment you wake up and doesn't stop until you get into the office.

Give a person a fish, and you feed them for a day; teach that person to use the Internet, and they won't bother you for weeks.

Accomplishing the impossible means your boss will add it to your job description.

I'm not lazy…

…I'm resting before
I get tired.

The only job where
you start at the top
is digging a hole.

A man's reputation rarely outlasts his money.

Time is an illusion,
lunchtime even more so.

Tomorrow is
the busiest day
of the week.

If it weren't for the last minute, I'd never get anything done.

What's the point of being a genius if you can't use it as an excuse for being unemployed?

If at first you don't
succeed, you're
about average.

A woman's work is never done, especially the part she asks her husband to do.

If work is so great, why did
the rich stop doing it?

Have you ever noticed that "the" and "IRS" spells "theirs"?

Opportunity often comes
disguised in the form
of misfortune,
or temporary defeat.

Many of life's failures are people who did not realize how close they were to success when they gave up.

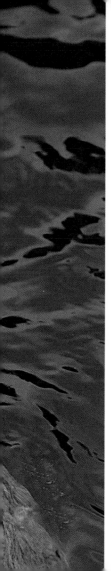

The minute you settle
for less than you deserve,
you get even less than
you settled for.

No matter how dark things seem to be, there are always possibilities.

Opportunities are like buses, there's always another one coming.

If two wrongs don't
make a right, try three.

If you think your boss is an idiot,
remember you wouldn't have
a job if he was any smarter.

Work hard for eight hours a day and you might just get promoted and have to work twelve hours a day.

Love is a highly desirable malfunction of the heart which weakens the brain, causes eyes to sparkle, cheeks to glow, blood pressure to rise, and lips to pucker.

Trip over love and
you can get up.
Fall in love and
you fall forever.

Love is the most important
thing in the world…

…and baseball's pretty good too.

Forget love...

...I'd rather fall in chocolate!

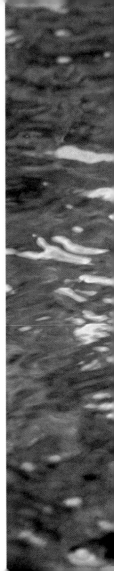

Love means
nothing in tennis,
but everything in life.

A husband will stand
by you through all the
troubles you wouldn't have
had if you'd stayed single.

Marriage, like insanity, means commitment.

Never marry for money…

…it's cheaper to borrow it.

Marriage changes passion— suddenly you're in bed with a relative.

A perfect wife is one who helps her husband with the dishes.

Football: A game devised
for padded cells played
in the open air.

Not knowing the
rules puts you on the
same level as the referee.

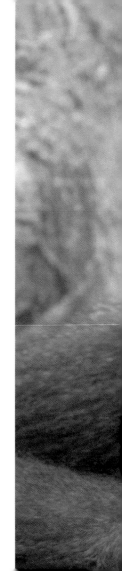

Monday is a dumb way to spend one seventh of your life.

If winning isn't everything,
why do they keep score?

Middle age is when you have a choice between two temptations and you choose the one that will get you home earlier.

Inflation is paying $20 for the haircut that cost $10 when you had hair.

I still have a full deck;
I just shuffle slower now.

It doesn't matter how high the mountain is, once you've climbed it you realize how low it was.

If you were happy every day of your life you wouldn't be a human being, you'd be a game show host.

If you don't look,
you won't find.

Obstacles are
opportunities waiting
to happen.

The greatest opportunities
are often disguised as
insurmountable obstacles.

Where there is a willing hand
and an open mind there
will always be a frontier.

Opportunity doesn't knock, it's there all the time, waiting for you to notice it.

Every day is an opportunity to make a new happy ending.

Believe and you can do anything.